REBECCA L. JOHNSON

CHERNOBYL'S WILD KINGDOM

LIFE IN THE DEAD ZONE

TWENTY-FIRST CENTURY BOOKS / MINNEAPOLIS

FOR ECW, WHO NEVER DOUBTS

Twenty-First Century Books
A division of Lerner Publishing Group, Inc.
241 First Avenue North
Minneapolis, MN 55401 USA

For reading levels and more information, look up this title at
www.lernerbooks.com.

Library of Congress Cataloging-in-Publication Data

Johnson, Rebecca L.
    Chernobyl's wild kingdom : life in the dead zone / by Rebecca
L. Johnson.
      p.   cm
    Includes bibliographical references and index.
    ISBN 978–1–4677–1154–8 (lib. bdg. : alk. paper)
    ISBN 978–1–4677–4791–2 (eBook).
    1. Chernobyl Nuclear Accident, Chornobyl, Ukraine, 1986—
Environmental aspects—Juvenile literature. 2. Radioecology—
Ukraine—Chornobyl Region—Juvenile literature. I. Title.
TK1362.U38J64 2015
590.9477'8—dc23   2013039471

Manufactured in the United States of America
1 – BP – 7/15/14

INTRODUCTION

The net across the window is nearly invisible in the faint morning light. Two barn swallows fly out of the abandoned farmhouse. They are caught in an instant, like moths in a spider's web.

Dr. Timothy Mousseau gently disentangles the swallows from the net's fine mesh. A biologist from the University of South Carolina, Mousseau has done this hundreds, probably thousands, of times. He slips the two swallows into small cloth bags and takes them to the makeshift laboratory he and his colleague, Danish ornithologist Dr. Anders Møller, have set up under the trees.

Møller deftly removes the first swallow from its sack, working quickly to minimize its stress. He weighs and measures the bird and takes a blood sample with a small hypodermic syringe. Then he painstakingly examines its body, peering at the plumage, gently lifting and extending the wings, and spreading the tail feathers. He inspects the beak, eyes, and feet.

After recording his observations, Møller eases the barn swallow into a narrow metal tube that he places inside a large scientific instrument. After a moment, numbers appear on the instrument's digital display. The numbers reveal something about the swallow that neither Møller nor Mousseau can see, no matter how closely they might look.

The numbers show how much radiation the barn swallow is giving off.

Elsewhere in the world, finding a radioactive bird might come as quite a shock. But not here. In this place, all the animals are radioactive. So are the trees, the grass, and the other plants. So are the mosses that cover the dilapidated buildings, and so are the mushrooms that sprout from the radioactive soil underfoot.

Welcome to Chernobyl, where the world's worst nuclear disaster spawned a strange wild kingdom of radioactive living things.

Biologist Timothy Mousseau and ornithologist Anders Møller study the effects of radiation on barn swallows and other birds at Chernobyl. They catch the birds in loose netting like this, take readings and measurements, and then release the birds.

CHAPTER 1
NUCLEAR NIGHTMARE

The story of Chernobyl's radioactive wildlife began almost three decades ago, in the early hours of April 26, 1986. On this late spring night, a moon just a few days past full cast a glow over the countryside of northern Ukraine. Lit by brilliant floodlights, the industrial complex of the Chernobyl Nuclear Power Plant was far brighter than the moon. The power plant operated around the clock. With its four nuclear reactors, the plant generated electricity for much of Ukraine, as well as parts of Belarus and southwestern Russia—republics that were part of the Soviet Union at that time. Just 2 miles (3.2 kilometers) north of the power plant was the small town of Pripyat. More than seventy-five hundred of its forty-five thousand inhabitants worked at the plant as engineers, technicians, and nuclear reactor operators.

A crew of radiation experts aboard a low-flying helicopter measures radiation levels at Chernobyl's Reactor Number 4 in the summer of 1986, just weeks after the initial explosion.

A TEST GOES TERRIBLY WRONG

A test of the cooling system of Chernobyl's Reactor Number 4 was scheduled for that late April night. Cool water flowing through pipes around the core helped maintain a safe temperature in the reactor. If the plant were to experience a power failure, however, the pumps that kept the coolant water flowing would stop and the core could overheat. If the temperature rose past a critical point, the core could melt and release dangerous ionizing radiation.

Emergency backup generators at Chernobyl were in place to keep the pumps running, if needed. But it would take about sixty seconds for the generators to become fully operational. For a nuclear reactor, a minute is a long time to be without properly flowing coolant water.

A highly radioactive vapor trail rises out of the rubble of Chernobyl's Reactor Number 4, just hours after the explosion on April 26, 1986.

POWER FROM NUCLEAR REACTIONS

The Chernobyl Nuclear Power Plant produced electricity by heating water to create pressurized steam. The steam traveled through pipes to large turbine generators, where the force of the steam hitting the turbine blades caused them to spin, generating electricity. The energy to heat the water came from nuclear reactions taking place in the reactor's center, or core.

In the core of a nuclear reactor, atoms of radioactive elements (typically uranium) are continuously splitting apart. Splitting atoms releases huge amounts of energy in the form of ionizing radiation. Unlike more familiar types of radiation, such as heat and light from the sun or microwaves from a microwave oven, ionizing radiation can harm—even kill—living things.

The goal of the April 26 test was to determine if, after the power was cut, the turbine blades of the main generator would keep spinning long enough on their own to produce sufficient electricity to keep the pumps going until the backup generators kicked in.

Similar tests had been performed at other nuclear reactors in the Soviet Union. But the Chernobyl plant manager, unlike managers at the other reactors, decided to carry out the test on Reactor Number 4 with many of the emergency safety systems turned off. This was a strange decision and, as it turned out, a disastrous one.

The test began at 1:23 a.m. At 1:23:04, technicians cut the power. The backup generators started up. The spinning turbine blades began to slow down. And then everything went wrong. Inside the reactor, nuclear reactions ran wild, releasing too much energy too quickly. The core temperature skyrocketed. The remaining water in the cooling system instantly turned to steam, causing an enormous increase in pressure. At 1:23:40, operators tried to reduce power in the reactor by triggering all the control rods—long tubes made of material that helps slow nuclear reactions—to descend into the core. But the rods jammed before they could slide into place; the overheated reactor had already begun to rupture. Violent tremors shook the power plant. At 1:23:58, Reactor Number 4 exploded.

According to the International Atomic Energy Agency, the explosion released four hundred times more radioactivity than the atomic bomb dropped on Hiroshima, Japan, during World War II (1939–1945). At least 50 tons (45.3 metric tons) of nuclear fuel vaporized, creating vast amounts of radioactive particles. The explosion tore off part of the roof of the reactor building and exposed what was left of the core to the open air. Extremely high levels of ionizing radiation streamed out in all directions. A glowing plume of searing hot radioactive particles, gases, and smoke billowed up from the damaged reactor and soared high into the sky. The heaviest particles began raining down as nuclear fallout on the surrounding landscape. Lighter particles, caught by the wind, headed away from Chernobyl through the darkness of that fateful night.

PRIPYAT IN PERIL

The explosion of Reactor Number 4 woke a few people in Pripyat. Most went back to sleep, but those who looked out their windows saw a glow coming from the plant. They assumed that it was an ordinary fire and that the plant's firefighting crews would quickly put it out. None of the townspeople suspected a nuclear accident or that invisible radioactive fallout was showering down on their community. And authorities didn't tell them, either.

CHERNOBYL'S REACH

Most of the radioactive material spewed from Reactor Number 4 fell on parts of northern Ukraine, southern Belarus, and southwestern Russia. Shifting winds carried varying amounts of radioactive fallout across much of Europe, including Scandinavia and as far west as the United Kingdom. The first alerts outside the Soviet Union of a nuclear accident came on April 27, 1986, from Sweden, where workers arriving for their shift at the Forsmark Nuclear Power Plant discovered radioactive particles on their clothing as they passed through detectors upon entering the building. High-level winds had spread radioactive particles from Chernobyl to Sweden (and to other parts of Europe) in less than twenty-four hours.

WARNING: RADIATION!

Ionizing radiation can be enormously harmful to living things, depending on the length of exposure to the radiation and the dose they receive. The radiation can damage molecules such as proteins and the genetic material deoxyribonucleic acid (DNA), all of which play important roles in cell processes. Cells are able to repair some amount of damage, but large doses of ionizing radiation can quickly overwhelm these cellular repair processes.

A person exposed to a massive dose of ionizing radiation, like the firefighters at Reactor Number 4, may suffer severe burns and develop radiation sickness that can be fatal in a matter of days or even hours. Somewhat smaller doses of radiation will damage DNA molecules that, if not repaired, can lead to genetic mutations, or permanent changes in DNA. If mutations occur in the DNA of body cells in tissues and organs, cancer may develop months or years after exposure. Genetic mutations in the DNA of reproductive cells (eggs and sperm) can be passed to future generations, potentially causing diseases, deformities, and other abnormalities.

Firefighting crews *were* battling blazes at the plant, trying valiantly to extinguish dozens of fires that had been ignited by the chunks of flaming radioactive material the reactor shot out. The firefighters did not know they were being exposed to massive doses of radiation, however. Authorities did not tell them or provide the crews with protective gear.

Why all the secrecy? Under Soviet rule, leaders in government and in government-run industries prized the appearance of being in complete control at all times. Even though a horrendous nuclear accident had just occurred, none of the power plant officials wanted to admit that anything was wrong. But the situation was very serious. The health and possibly even the lives of thousands of people were at risk.

The firefighters battling the blazes at the power plant were exposed to tremendously high levels of ionizing radiation, receiving doses between six thousand and ten thousand millisieverts (mSv). Many died within weeks of the accident. In Pripyat, radiation levels

A sign in the Exclusion Zone surrounding the Chernobyl power plant warns of radiation.

weren't as intense, but they continued to increase as the nuclear fallout descended hour after hour, silent and invisible, from the sky.

EVACUATION

Saturday morning dawned bright and sunny in Pripyat. People went about their normal lives, still unaware of the radiation threat. They went shopping and to the park. Mothers pushed babies in strollers, and children who had Saturday classes went to school.

Around midmorning, police and soldiers in radiation suits and gas masks arrived. Trucks fitted out with large water tanks began washing the streets. Sixteen-year-old Pripyat resident Vitaly Petrenko remembered how "some sort of foam covered the pavements and roads . . . [and] fire engines were endlessly watering the streets." When residents asked what was going on, they were told it was just a drill. Children played in the glistening foam. No one warned them that it was saturated with dangerous radioactive particles.

RADIATION DOSES AND THEIR EFFECTS

Event	Radiation dose, in millisieverts (mSv)
Single dose, fatal within days or weeks	10,000
One-minute exposure to the Chernobyl nuclear reactor core just after the explosion	5,000
Average dose received by Chernobyl firefighters and plant workers who died within thirty days	6,000
Single dose that causes temporary, nonfatal radiation sickness	1,000
Accumulated dose that may cause a fatal cancer to develop sometime after exposure	1,000
Average dose received by area residents who were evacuated after the Chernobyl accident	350
Dose received during a full-body CT scan	9
Average annual dose received by airline crews flying a polar route from New York to Tokyo	9
Average annual dose of natural background radiation received by the general population worldwide	2
Dose from a spinal X-ray	1.5
Dose from a dental X-ray	0.01

This chart—based on information available from the World Nuclear Association, United Nations Scientific Committee on the Effects of Atomic Radiation (UNSCEAR), and radiologyinfo.org—compares the potential effects on living things of different amounts of radiation measured in millisieverts (mSv). The millisievert is a scientific unit of measurement named for Swedish physicist Rolf Maximilian Sievert, known for his work on the biological effects of radiation.

Some residents climbed onto the rooftops of apartment buildings to get a better view of the fire at the power plant. After a while, these onlookers became weak and nauseous. Their skin darkened, a radiation effect known as a nuclear tan. Suspicion began to mount that this was no ordinary fire.

As radiation levels continued to rise, officials finally decided to evacuate Pripyat. Still, they waited another day to act. It was not until 2:00 p.m. on Sunday, April 27, that eleven hundred evacuation buses rumbled into the town. Residents scrambled aboard the buses, taking only what they could carry. Three hours later, Pripyat was a radioactive ghost town.

After evacuation, the town of Pripyat, Ukraine, became—and has remained—a ghost town. The rusted and abandoned remains of human activity are the only signs of a community founded in 1970 specifically to house nuclear power plant employees.

THE LIQUIDATORS

As authorities emptied Pripyat of its inhabitants, helicopters dropped countless loads of sand, clay, lead, and other minerals onto the exposed core of the power plant in an attempt to smother the nuclear fire. The core's flaming red eye finally flickered out ten days later.

More than six hundred thousand emergency workers known as liquidators came from all over the Soviet Union to clean up the disaster site. Teams of liquidators cleared the most intensely radioactive debris from what was left of the roof of Reactor Number 4, shoveling and tossing it onto the buried core. Radiation levels were so high that the workers were allowed onto the rooftop for only a very short time. They absorbed a lifetime's worth of radiation in seconds.

Tens of thousands of liquidators worked for six months to construct an enormous steel and concrete enclosure over the fiercely radioactive remains of the damaged reactor. Nicknamed the Sarcophagus (coffin), the thick-walled structure formed a shield over the buried nuclear core to help prevent radiation from escaping.

In the fall of 1986, liquidators remove radioactive debris from the roof of Chernobyl's Reactor Number 4 in single sixty-second shifts. In that time, they received what was considered the maximum dose of radiation that anyone should be exposed to in a lifetime. In reality, these workers were exposed to far more than that.

CHERNOBYL'S EFFECTS ON PEOPLE

How many people were harmed by Chernobyl's nuclear meltdown? Answers vary tremendously, depending on the source. According to the United Nations Scientific Committee on the Effects of Atomic Radiation, the meltdown led to 134 confirmed cases of acute radiation sickness. These were primarily firefighters and power plant workers exposed to high doses of radiation immediately after the accident. Within a few months, 31 of these people died.

The longer-term effects, however, are still uncertain and highly controversial. A 2005 report issued by the Chernobyl Forum—an international group of experts assembled by the United Nations, the World Health Organization, and the International Atomic Energy Agency—estimated four thousand people would eventually die from leukemia and other radiation-induced cancers as a direct result of the Chernobyl nuclear disaster. Critics argued that key information was not included in preparing the report. If it had been, they claimed, the estimated number of future cancer-related deaths would be forty thousand. The environmental activist group Greenpeace International conducted its own study, involving more than fifty scientists from many different countries. Their estimate? At least ninety-three thousand people would ultimately die of radiation-induced cancers from Chernobyl.

What has been confirmed so far? In Ukraine at least four thousand cases of thyroid cancer among people exposed to Chernobyl's radioactive fallout as children or as young adults have been documented. (The thyroid gland is very sensitive to radiation damage that can lead to cancer, and this sensitivity is especially high in children and adolescents.) Israeli and Ukrainian researchers reported in 2001 that children born to liquidators after their exposure at Chernobyl had very high levels of mutations in their DNA. And at least ninety thousand of the two hundred thousand liquidators still alive in 2013 were suffering from serious health problems that could be related to their radiation exposure.

Four years after the Chernobyl disaster, government authorities were still relocating families such as this couple to "clean" areas away from the Exclusion Zone. While tens of thousands of people were exposed to dangerous radioactive fallout as a result of the accident, scientists and medical experts do not agree on the long-term effects of that exposure.

Other liquidators worked in the countryside around the power plant. They used bulldozers to scrape off the top few inches of radioactive soil, which they packed into steel drums and buried deep in the ground. In a desperate and fruitless decontamination effort, they washed the streets and empty buildings of Pripyat and the small towns and villages that had been evacuated around Chernobyl.

Near the power plant, acres of pine forest had been showered with radiation so intense that the trees died within days and turned an eerie, rusty red color. Liquidators cut down most of the trees in what they called the Red Forest and buried them in long, shallow, gravelike trenches.

THE EXCLUSION ZONE

When the liquidators had done as much as they could do, they abandoned their trucks and bulldozers—even their helicopters. The vehicles were too radioactive to be used again. Military personnel set up a perimeter around the power plant with a radius of 18.6 miles (30 km) from Reactor Number 4. Hastily fenced off, this forbidden area was officially known as the Exclusion Zone, or the Zone of Alienation. But many people called it the Dead Zone. Roadblocks with armed guards controlled all access to this radioactive no-man's-land.

The Exclusion Zone was essentially abandoned. The few horses and cows left behind soon died of radiation sickness. Many wild animals died too, although no one knew exactly how many. Radiation levels were so high in the Zone it seemed likely that all the wildlife there would eventually be wiped out. Most people, including many scientists, assumed that Chernobyl's Exclusion Zone would become a barren wasteland—an empty, lifeless landscape like something from a science fiction story about the end of the world.

But that's not what happened. To almost everyone's surprise, life in the Zone wasn't extinguished at all.

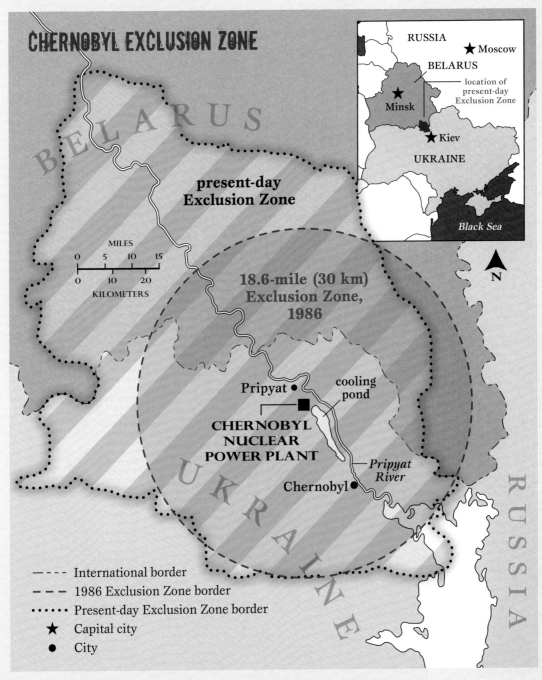

CHERNOBYL EXCLUSION ZONE

BELARUS

RUSSIA

BELARUS
★ Moscow

location of present-day Exclusion Zone

★ Minsk

★ Kiev

UKRAINE

Black Sea

present-day Exclusion Zone

MILES

0   5   10   15

0   10   20
KILOMETERS

18.6-mile (30 km) Exclusion Zone, 1986

N

Pripyat ●

cooling pond

CHERNOBYL NUCLEAR POWER PLANT

Pripyat River

Chernobyl ●

UKRAINE

RUSSIA

– – – – International border
– – – 1986 Exclusion Zone border
••••• Present-day Exclusion Zone border
★ Capital city
● City

Initially, the Exclusion Zone lay within a radius of 18.6 miles (30 km) from the Chernobyl Nuclear Power Plant. More accurate measurements of radiation levels in the surrounding countryside led scientists to expand the Zone to include larger areas of both Ukraine and Belarus.

CHAPTER 2
WILD KINGDOM

More than a quarter century after the nuclear accident at Chernobyl, access to the Exclusion Zone is still limited and strictly controlled. With more accurate measurements of radiation levels across the region, the Zone has been expanded several times since it was first established. Currently, it is an irregularly shaped area about the size of South Carolina, split roughly through the middle, east to west, by the border between Ukraine and Belarus. Occasionally, official guides lead tours of small numbers of journalists and tourists to places where the radiation is relatively low. Most of the other visitors are scientists, who have greater freedom to travel wherever they want in the area.

No one can enter the Zone, though, without first passing through a security checkpoint along the perimeter fence. Checkpoint guards scrutinize permits and other official documents required for entry. If everything is in order, the guards lift the bars that block the road, granting access to one of the strangest places on Earth.

Beyond the fence, the vegetation is lush and green. In some places, trees grow right up to the edge of the road. Their branches arch overhead to form a leafy canopy so dense it filters out some of the sunlight and casts deep shadows all around. Clumps of grass and weeds sprout from cracks and potholes in the crumbling asphalt, and wildflowers bloom along the roadside.

The stillness is almost unnerving. No traffic noises or sounds of construction. No music blaring or children laughing. The silence is broken only by birds calling from the treetops, leaves rustling in the breeze, and the *click, click, click* of dosimeters registering the radiation from the pavement, the soil, and the nearest plants.

LIFE IN ABUNDANCE

The potholed remnants of the road wind deeper into the Zone. The air is cool and moist, heavy with the scent of vegetation and damp earth. Suddenly, there is movement in the trees. With a loud snort, a wild boar steps into the open, followed by her striped piglets. The mother boar stares for a moment and then begins rooting in the dirt beside the road with her strong snout and sharp tusks. Her offspring crowd around her, scrabbling for the mushrooms and roots she unearths.

Wild boars were scarce in the region around Chernobyl before the accident at Reactor Number 4. "After the accident, their population grew considerably," says Ukrainian biologist Dr. Sergey Gaschak.

Stray dogs play in the shadow of Chernobyl's Reactor Number 4. A new protective structure to cover the damaged reactor is under construction, as the existing sarcophagus is deteriorating and unstable.

"Now, they are common." Gaschak is the deputy director of the International Radioecology Laboratory in Slavutych, Ukraine, located just outside the Zone. After coming to Chernobyl as a liquidator, he stayed to study the animals. The size of the wild boar population varies from year to year, but Gaschak thinks the Zone is home to at least one thousand boars.

And they are not alone.

Sharing the thick forests and green meadows with the boars are thousands of red and roe deer and a large population of moose. Foxes and lynx slink through the shadowy undergrowth. Estimates vary, but as many as two hundred wolves may be living in the Chernobyl Exclusion Zone, grouped into perhaps a dozen wolf packs. In addition to these large mammals are many smaller ones, including beavers, Eurasian badgers, mink, otters, hare, raccoons, bats, mice, and other rodents. The Zone also has hundreds of species of birds, reptiles, amphibians, and insects.

RADIATION DETECTORS

Scientists who work in Chernobyl's Exclusion Zone bring many different kinds of equipment with them, depending on the type of research they are doing. Two items, however, are essential to every researcher: radiation maps and radiation dosimeters. The maps show radiation levels in detail across the landscape. The nuclear fallout from Reactor Number 4 fell much more heavily in some places than others, creating a patchwork of hot spots separated by less radioactive areas. When traveling in the Zone, following the maps carefully is essential. Without the maps, it is impossible to tell a dangerously radioactive place from one that is far less contaminated.

A radiation dosimeter is a small portable instrument that, like a Geiger counter, detects and measures ionizing radiation. On a small screen, a dosimeter shows the amount of radiation it is sensing. A dosimeter also makes a clicking sound like a Geiger counter: the more rapid the clicks, the more intense the radiation. If the clicks come so quickly that they blend together to create screeching white noise, you're in a hot spot, and staying long in that place is not a good idea.

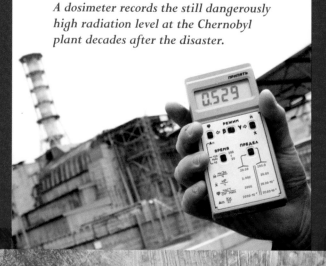

A dosimeter records the still dangerously high radiation level at the Chernobyl plant decades after the disaster.

Sergey Gaschak's photographs of a red fox (top) *and a moose* (bottom) *in the Exclusion Zone. More moose live within the Exclusion Zone than anywhere else in Ukraine.*

Gaschak has spent more than twenty years studying the Zone's amazing wildlife recovery. Along with other scientists, he has documented nearly everything that lives and grows in the Ukrainian side of the Zone. The list is long and impressive, with more than 320 different kinds of vertebrates (animals with backbones), including 186 kinds of birds and fifty-five types of mammals. Among these are several rare and endangered species. One is the white-tailed eagle. Two others are the barbastelle bat, not seen around Chernobyl for more than fifty years, and the greater noctule bat, which hasn't been spotted anywhere in Ukraine for at least sixty years. In addition to all the animals, more than fifteen hundred species of plants, mosses, and lichens are now growing in what amounts to ground zero of the nuclear accident.

In his explorations of the Zone, Gaschak has spent a lot of time looking at wildlife. He has seen moose with newborn calves crossing marshes, knee-deep in mud saturated with the remains of nuclear fallout. He has seen wild boars rooting for mushrooms around the

PRZEWALSKI'S HORSES

In the late 1990s, Ukrainian officials released thirty-one Przewalski's (sheh-VAHL-skeez) horses into the Zone. Long ago, these compact, sturdy wild horses roamed across much of eastern Europe, Russia, Mongolia, and parts of China. Since 1879, however, they have been extinct in the wild in Europe and Russia and survived as a species there only through captive breeding programs. The horses released into the Zone came from a Ukrainian reserve and a zoo. The hope was that in the isolated environment of the Zone, the horses would successfully reproduce in a more natural setting.

The Przewalski's horses seemed to flourish within the boundaries of the Zone. By 2003 the size of the herd had more than doubled. Photographs of the horses running free through the meadows around the power plant came to symbolize the dramatic recovery that wildlife was making in the aftermath of the nuclear disaster.

Poachers have killed several dozen Przewalski's horses in the past few years, reducing their numbers dramatically. Despite the fences and the checkpoints—even the threat of radiation—the animals within the Zone are not entirely safe from people.

gnarled roots of trees that have been growing in radioactive soil for years. He has even spotted birds nesting in the nooks and crannies of the concrete sarcophagus that surrounds Reactor Number 4.

To help record when, where, and what animals are doing, Gaschak has set up hidden cameras at different locations around the Zone. Each camera is equipped with a motion detector. When an animal gets close enough to trigger the detector, the camera automatically takes a picture. Day and night, these hidden cameras document the activities of wildlife—feeding, hunting, and reproducing—in a radioactive world.

Many of Gaschak's photos could easily pass for snapshots of a pristine wilderness. How could a place so contaminated by nuclear fallout become a seeming paradise for wildlife?

NATURE'S COMEBACK

Some scientists think that during the first twenty-four hours after Reactor Number 4 exploded, radiation levels were high enough in places like the Red Forest to kill every single mammal there. But with

Three adult and one juvenile (third from left) *Przewalski's horses kept a close eye on Sergey Gaschak as he snapped this photograph. Although they are wild, some of the Przewalski's horses in the Exclusion Zone seem to have little fear of people.*

RADIONUCLIDES AND HALF-LIVES

During radioactive decay, a radionuclide spontaneously gives off energy in the form of either high-energy rays (typically gamma rays) or high-energy particles (two of the most common are alpha and beta particles). If it gives off particles, the radionuclide changes into a different element. For example, americium-241, a radionuclide used in smoke detectors, releases alpha particles as it decays. It becomes neptunium-237 in the process.

Scientists measure radioactive decay in terms of half-life. The half-life of a radionuclide is the time it takes for half a given amount of that radionuclide to decay. Every type of radionuclide has a unique half-life. Half-lives range from a fraction of a second to billions of years.

time, the amount of radionuclides (radioactive particles) began to decrease through the process of radioactive decay.

Iodine-131 was among the first to disappear from the Exclusion Zone—and from wherever else Chernobyl's nuclear fallout had landed. This radionuclide is especially dangerous to vertebrates, including people, because the thyroid gland quickly absorbs it. The thyroid gland produces hormones, substances that regulate the activity of all body cells. A large dose of iodine-131 can destroy the thyroid gland, and lower doses can lead to thyroid cancer. Some of the cattle and horses left behind in the Zone died of iodine-131 exposure. From later forensic analyses, scientists discovered that the animals' thyroids took up so much of this radioactive substance that the glands simply disintegrated, eventually leading to death. The same thing probably happened to some of the Zone's wild animals.

As destructive as it is, iodine-131 has a relatively short half-life: a little more than eight days. Roughly three months after Chernobyl's nuclear accident, nearly all the iodine-131 released by the explosion had decayed into xenon-131, a harmless element. Other radionuclides with longer half-lives were also decaying, although much more slowly. As months and years passed, radiation levels throughout the Zone steadily decreased. By the mid-1990s, they were one thousand times lower than they had been immediately after the accident. Animals were surviving at least long enough to reproduce, and populations of living things began to increase.

A RADIOACTIVE NATURE PRESERVE

The almost complete absence of people was key to the wildlife recovery. In the first few months after the accident, authorities evacuated an estimated 116,000 people from the Zone. In addition to Pripyat, several towns and more than one hundred villages were emptied of their inhabitants. Many villages were simply abandoned. Some were so radioactive they were bulldozed into piles of rubble.

When the people left, so did many threats to wildlife. For example, hunting, fishing, and trapping disappeared. Once-busy roads were empty, and animals were no longer at risk of being hit by cars and trucks. Farming and forestry ceased, along with the use of pesticides, herbicides, and other chemicals toxic to living things. Industries shut down and industrial pollution no longer flowed into lakes, rivers, and streams.

The survival of plant life also helped make the Zone more livable by reshaping what people had left behind. Vines covered abandoned houses and farmsteads. Seeds of bushes and trees sprouted in places where people had lived and worked and played. Lands once drained for agriculture reverted to wetlands. Wild grasses and other plants took over agricultural fields. These changes created the types of habitats— marshlands, meadows, and forests with dense undergrowth—that had been in short supply before Chernobyl's nuclear accident.

Local scientists reported seeing unexpectedly large numbers of animals in the Exclusion Zone around the year 1995. By around 2000, it was obvious that more wild animals were living in the Zone than outside it. The Chernobyl Forum's 2005 report noted, "The Exclusion Zone has paradoxically become a unique sanctuary for biodiversity." Although no one planned it, Chernobyl's Exclusion Zone had become one of the largest nature preserves in Europe.

INVISIBLE THREAT

But what about the radiation?

While radiation levels have dropped as a result of radioactive

CHERNOBYL'S SELF-SETTLERS

Although it is technically against the law, a few hundred people have returned to their former homes in the Exclusion Zone in abandoned villages. About 80 percent of these self-settlers, as the Ukrainian government calls them, are elderly women in their seventies and eighties. Most came back within a few years of evacuation. They prefer to face the risk of radiation-related illnesses than to permanently abandon the places where they grew up and raised their families. They survive by growing vegetables, harvesting fruit from old orchards, and raising a few animals such as pigs for food. Relatives from outside the Zone visit periodically to bring food, medicines, and other necessities.

decay, the Exclusion Zone remains the most radioactive environment on Earth. It was so contaminated by nuclear fallout that it won't be completely safe for people to live there for hundreds of years. Hot spots such as the Red Forest will likely be uninhabitable by humans for an even longer period of time. Yet, the Zone's animals don't seem to be aware of the danger all around them. Some live and breed in places where dosimeters and Geiger counters still register high levels of ionizing radiation.

Not only do the animals live with this chronic, relatively low-level background radiation day in and day out, they are also exposed to radiation internally. Over the years, rain has washed much of the nuclear fallout into the soil and the muddy bottoms of lakes and streams. Yet, two radionuclides in particular—cesium-137 and strontium-90, each with half-lives of about thirty years—continue to cycle *through* the Zone's living things. Through their roots, plants take up these radionuclides from the soil. Animals that eat plants, and animals that eat plant eaters, take the radionuclides into their bodies, where they become incorporated into cells, tissues, and organs. Cesium-137 tends to settle in muscle and other soft tissues. Strontium-90 settles in bones and teeth. The bones of some of the large animal carcasses in the Zone are so radioactive that some scientists prefer to wear gloves to handle them.

Zina Guzienko chose to return to her evacuated village in the Exclusion Zone.

"All the animals living in the Chernobyl Exclusion Zone consume radionuclides—they have no choice," Gaschak says. "But the amount of radionuclide intake depends on the kind of foods they are eating. Some animals are more contaminated, some less." Animals that eat lichens and mushrooms—which take up and concentrate radionuclides even more than plants do—are usually the most contaminated. Internal radiation exposure is particularly hazardous to living things. Radionuclides are in direct contact with cells, constantly releasing ionizing radiation that can destroy those cells or cause mutations in their DNA.

All the same, the abundant wildlife in the Zone looks remarkably normal. The animals seem to be healthy. Many species appear to be thriving.

But are they? Are the mammals, birds, and other animals living around Chernobyl immune to the damaging effects of radiation, both in their environment and inside their bodies? Or is the radiation harming them in ways that aren't easy to see or that are taking a long time to show up?

Finding answers to these questions has proved to be challenging—and controversial.

CHAPTER 3
RADIOACTIVE RODENTS

The bank vole may be one of the world's cutest animals. Around Chernobyl, this little rodent also has the distinction of being one of the most radioactive.

"We call them screamers," says Texas Tech University biologist Dr. Robert Baker. "When you hold a Geiger counter up to some of them, it makes a screaming sound because the voles are so radioactive, especially if they've been eating lichens."

Just how radioactive are they? In a single year, Chernobyl's most contaminated bank voles receive a radiation dose that is equivalent to a person getting sixty-five thousand chest X-rays in the same amount of time. Yet, the voles don't look the least bit sick. They're not deformed or crippled. In fact, they look perfectly normal. Trying to figure out why these tiny mammals are doing so well while living in such a radioactive environment has kept Baker and his colleagues busy for more than twenty years.

Baker made his first trip to Chernobyl in 1994 with fellow biologist Dr. Ronald Chesser, also from Texas Tech. On one of their first excursions into the Zone, the two scientists got unnervingly close to the Sarcophagus covering the buried nuclear core. "When I first walked out there, about 300 meters [328 yards] from Reactor 4, I got my Geiger counter out and put it down on the ground, and it went crazy. Then I held it up to my chest and it did the same thing. I thought to myself: 'There's that much radiation going through me.' I was concerned that I was doing something to myself that I probably shouldn't be. But after a while, you get used to it."

Baker and Chesser wanted to know how small mammals living in some of the Zone's most contaminated places were faring. The Red Forest was one of their study sites. Clad in boots and protective coveralls, they walked among the mounds of buried radiation-blasted pine trees while their dosimeters gave out steady streams of rapid clicks. To the scientists' surprise, healthy-looking birch trees were growing where the pine trees had once stood. And lots of little creatures were scurrying around.

Baker and Chesser set up traps and captured dozens of voles and mice. The voles, in particular, were astonishingly radioactive, with high levels of strontium-90 in their bones and of cesium-137 in their soft tissues. Yet, not a single animal the scientists captured was deformed in any way. The little rodents showed no signs of lesions or tumors. "It was totally unexpected," says Baker. "I really thought that the life-forms on the ground, the little mammals, would probably be heavily compromised [harmed by the radiation] in some way." But they didn't seem to be. Their apparent good health was almost hard to believe.

Some bank voles living in Chernobyl's Exclusion Zone are extremely radioactive because they spend a lot of time burrowing in soil and eating foods such as lichens that tend to accumulate large amounts of radionuclides. Yet the little rodents appear to be quite normal, with few genetic mutations.

CHERNOBYL'S "MONSTERS"

On dry land, bank voles in the Exclusion Zone will make a Geiger counter scream. Deep down in the waters of a lake beside the Chernobyl power plant, a certain type of fish will do the same thing— a very big highly radioactive fish.

The lake is the power plant's former cooling pond, the source for the millions of gallons of water used to cool the nuclear reactors. When the power plant was built, the cooling pond was stocked with many different kinds of fish, including wels catfish, the largest species of freshwater catfish in Europe.

The cooling pond was heavily contaminated by radioactive material released by the Reactor Number 4 explosion. Year after year since the accident, rains have continued to wash radionuclides from the land into the water. The murky ooze of sediment at the bottom of the cooling pond is full of cesium-137 and strontium-90 as well as plutonium-239, which has a half-life of twenty-four thousand years. Wels catfish are at the top of the food chain in the cooling pond. Because everything they eat is contaminated with radionuclides, the catfish are highly radioactive themselves.

Sightings of enormous catfish in the cooling pond sparked rumors that the high levels of radiation had turned the fish into gigantic, mutated monsters. Scientists put the rumors to rest. The catfish have no visible mutations or obvious deformities. They just seem monstrous because they are so much bigger than humans expect to see. When people were around to catch them, they typically caught the fish early in the animal's life cycle, when it was fairly small. But left undisturbed since the accident, some of the catfish have grown to their full adult size of nearly 18 feet (5.5 meters) in length.

LOOKING FOR MUTATIONS

The scientists knew, however, that simply because animals look normal on the outside doesn't mean they might not have abnormalities in their genetic material. Because bank voles were the most radioactive species they had collected, Baker and Chesser reasoned that voles would probably be as likely as any animal in the Zone to show signs of DNA mutations.

On subsequent trips to Chernobyl, Baker, Chesser, and a team of assistants collected more voles from the Exclusion Zone, as well as from uncontaminated, clean sites outside the Zone. Back in a laboratory, the scientists isolated cells from both groups of animals. They extracted DNA from those cells and analyzed it for mutations. The researchers repeated the

Robert Baker (above) *collects tissue samples from small rodents that live outside the Exclusion Zone. By comparing the DNA of voles and mice that live outside the Zone to those that live inside it, Baker can spot genetic mutations that may be the result of radiation exposure.*

DNA analyses several times, using different techniques. Although they had expected to find lots of mutations in voles from the highly radioactive sites, they found very few. So few, in fact, that Baker and his colleagues concluded that voles from contaminated sites and voles from clean sites exhibited no significant genetic differences. Despite the high level of ionizing radiation to which voles in the Zone were exposed, they appeared to be genetically and physically normal.

This was a remarkable finding. Humans exposed to the same level of radiation the voles were receiving in the Red Forest would almost certainly have genetic mutations in their DNA. How were the voles and other rodents able to tolerate so much radiation? Were they somehow resistant to its damaging effects?

THE HORMESIS HYPOTHESIS

Baker and his colleagues thought it was possible that voles and other small rodents in the Zone might be showing something called radiation hormesis. The hormesis hypothesis suggests that relatively small amounts of something harmful can actually be helpful to living things by making them more resistant to damage or disease. A few scientists, including Baker, think regular exposure to relatively low doses of radiation can stimulate cells to repair damage to DNA more effectively, canceling out radiation's negative effects. "In radiation hormesis, cells are overreacting to a challenge," says Baker. "And by overreacting, they are protecting themselves from the damage you might otherwise expect."

Radiation hormesis is a controversial idea. Most scientists remain unconvinced that any amount of radiation exposure is helpful to living things. Yet, the results from a few studies on humans are intriguing. For example, nuclear power plant workers are continually exposed to low levels of radiation on the job. In studies carried out in Canada and the United Kingdom, researchers found that nuclear power plant workers have cancer rates that are lower than the national averages in those two nations.

A mouse (Microtus) *wears a small dosimeter around its neck for an experiment. The mouse was released into the Red Forest and retrapped a few days later. The dosimeter measured the amount of radiation the mouse had received.*

Results like these have sparked interest in looking more closely at how long-term exposure to relatively low-dose radiation affects living things. Chernobyl's Exclusion Zone provided the Texas Tech scientists with an ideal natural laboratory in which to test this idea.

So in 2005, Baker and Brenda Rodgers, one of his PhD students, brought some very special mice to Chernobyl. The mice were a strain bred to be unusually sensitive to ionizing radiation. The scientists took the mice into the Red Forest and placed them in open-air cages on the ground. For several weeks, the mice lived in the forest, exposed to the radiation in the soil and vegetation all around them. Then the scientists took the mice to a laboratory, where they exposed them to a short burst of very high radiation. They also gave a group of clean mice, with no previous radiation exposure, the same burst of intense radiation.

Afterward, the science team examined the cells of both groups of mice. The results? The mice that had lived in the Red Forest and been exposed to the background radiation for several weeks had less DNA damage than the mice that had received only the high-dose radiation burst. The cells of the Red Forest–exposed mice also contained greater amounts of proteins that repair broken strands of DNA and otherwise protect cells from radiation damage. The scientists felt the experiment provided pretty strong evidence for radiation hormesis. Weeks of exposure to relatively low levels of radiation seemed to help the mice's cells survive a much higher radiation dose later on.

Is this what is happening with the bank voles and other small rodents in the Zone? Is their constant exposure to the radiation stimulating their cells to work harder to repair any damage? Is this the secret to their remarkably healthy appearance? Baker thinks it is: "We believe the bank voles up-regulate [turn on their cellular repair mechanisms] all the time."

But is what's happening with bank voles true for other animals in the Zone? Can all the wildlife shrug off radiation as easily as voles appear to do? Baker takes a positive view, saying, "If bank voles exhibit radiation hormesis, and it's canceling out the harmful effects of radiation in their bodies, I'm pretty comfortable thinking it might be happening in other species." Biologists Mousseau and Møller would be the first to disagree.

RADIORESISTANT PLANTS

Like most of the animals in the Exclusion Zone, the plants there have also made a remarkable recovery. With the exception of a few species such as Scots pine (the type of pine trees originally in the Red Forest), most of the Zone's plants are growing and reproducing relatively well. Scientists have been surprised by this.

Katarina Klubicova is a plant scientist at the Institute of Plant Genetics and Biotechnology at the Slovak Academy of Sciences in Slovakia. Along with fellow plant scientist Dr. Martin Hajduch and several other colleagues, she has been carrying out experiments on soybeans, hoping to uncover the secret to the plant's apparent resistance to radiation in the Zone. Beginning in 2008, the researchers planted soybeans in small plots both inside and outside the Zone. Plants inside the Zone were exposed to levels of cesium-137 and strontium-90 that were many times higher than levels to which plants outside the Zone are exposed. In the Zone, the scientists wore protective suits, gloves, safety glasses, and respirators to reduce exposure to radionuclides in soil and dust raised by their activities.

The researchers tracked soybean growth in both locations and harvested the seeds the plants produced. Seeds from soybean plants grown in the Zone were smaller than seeds from plants grown outside the Zone, and they were radioactive. Nevertheless, the Zone-grown seeds appeared to be normal in every other respect. When planted, they grew into normal-looking soybean plants.

When Klubicova analyzed proteins in Zone-grown seeds, she found important clues to why soybean plants grow as well as they do in a radioactive environment. Compared to normal soybean seeds, those of Zone-grown soybeans contained much less of a protein called beta-conglycinin. Plants are known to use their stores of beta-conglycinin to reverse damage caused by toxic metals (both strontium and cesium are toxic metal elements).

Zone-grown seeds also contained higher than normal levels of cysteine synthase, a protein that helps plants tolerate the stress caused by the presence of toxic metals in their cells and tissues. Based on these findings, Klubicova concludes that soybeans are using and producing proteins in specific ways to protect themselves from the negative effects of radionuclides. Whether other types of plants in the Exclusion Zone use a similar strategy is not clear, but scientists are working to find out.

A sign (top) *marks the entrance to one of the research plots inside the Exclusion Zone where plant scientist Katarina Klubicova and her colleagues grow soybeans* (inset) *to study the effects of radiation on the plants.*

CHAPTER 4
A SWALLOW'S TALE

In the late nineteenth and early twentieth centuries, miners used canaries to determine whether a coal mine was free of deadly carbon monoxide gas following an explosion or underground fire. Miners wearing gas masks slowly entered the mines carrying canaries in birdcages. If the birds looked and behaved normally, the miners felt the air in the mine was safe to breathe. If the birds started to struggle and gasp for breath, it was a sure sign that the air was contaminated with carbon monoxide. In short, the condition of the birds warned of an invisible danger. For scientists Mousseau and Møller, barn swallows are the canaries as the two researchers study the effects of radiation in Chernobyl's Exclusion Zone.

The two men first visited Chernobyl together in 2000. Both had visited Chernobyl in previous years and felt there were many interesting scientific questions that they might study together in this region of high radioactivity. They had heard and read the official claims that radiation was having little or no effect on the wildlife but were skeptical given the size of this nuclear disaster. They wanted to investigate the situation for themselves to determine whether or not any animals had in some way adapted to this radioactive environment. The animals they initially decided to study were barn swallows.

"We chose to look at barn swallows in the Zone because they've been well-studied in other parts of the world," explains Mousseau.

"They typically breed inside buildings, nesting together to form colonies. Barn swallows are migratory and return to the same site to breed year after year, making it possible for us to track individuals and their offspring over time."

Mousseau and Møller visited abandoned villages throughout the Zone, inspecting houses and barns for the presence of barn swallows. In these and any other building where they found nesting swallows, they strung nets across open windows and doorways to catch birds as they exited and entered the buildings to build their nests or to forage for insects to feed their young.

For each bird, the scientists took radiation measurements. First, they used an instrument similar to a Geiger counter to determine the radiation at the site where the bird was captured. Next, the scientists measured radiation in the bird itself, slipping the animal into a metal tube and then into a

Photos by Timothy Mousseau show the normal throat coloration of a male barn swallow (top) *in comparison to areas of albinistic (white) feathers on the throat and above the beak of another male swallow* (bottom). *Mousseau and his colleague Anders Møller attribute the partial albinism to radiation exposure.*

portable gamma spectrometer. This instrument detects radioactivity and measures the type of radionuclides inside the bird's body that are emitting the radiation.

"The second measure is of the amount of radioactive particles inside the bird's body," explains Møller. "For this, we use an instrument [the spectrometer] shielded by several hundred kilograms of lead so it measures only what is inside the bird, not what is outside." The test doesn't take long and doesn't harm the birds in any way. "They sit happily inside this 'lead cave' for about ten minutes while we measure how radioactive they are," says Mousseau.

Many of the swallows were quite radioactive. Like other animals in the Zone, barn swallows take radionuclides into their bodies through their food. Swallows also build their nests out of the Zone's mud, which is usually heavily contaminated with radionuclides.

After weighing, measuring, and scrutinizing every inch of a swallow's small body, the scientists attached a tiny identifying band on one of its legs and released it. Some birds were also equipped with miniature dosimeters on their leg bands so that the scientists could measure the external radiation experienced by individual swallows. They repeated this process dozens of times a day, at different sites. Some sites were in radioactive hot spots, while others were in parts of the Zone where radiation levels are lower.

From the very start of their investigation, Mousseau and Møller discovered that, unlike bank voles, many barn swallows in the Zone did not look normal. The heads, backs, and throats of barn swallows are usually dark blue or chestnut brown, with no white. But these birds had unusual small patches of white feathers on their bodies as a result of a lack of pigment. This lack of pigment is known as albinism, which in nature is rare. Yet among barn swallows in the Zone, it was quite common. The scientists suspected radiation was to blame.

Albinism can occur when melanocytes (pigment-producing cells) are damaged. Melanocytes are particularly vulnerable to the effects of radiation. They die more easily than other types of body cells when exposed to radionuclides. "Up to 20 percent of barn swallows in the Zone show some evidence of melanocyte death," says Mousseau.

IT PAYS TO BE SAFE

After working in the Chernobyl Exclusion Zone for many years, Møller and Mousseau have gotten used to being in an environment where invisible ionizing radiation is all around them, all the time. They have developed good habits to stay safe.

"The first priority is always safety," says Møller. "So it is a no-no to suck on grass straws, lick your fingers, and other similar kinds of behavior. And we *never* sit on the ground."

In highly contaminated areas, the researchers wear rubber boots and white suits made of thin, flexible fabric to prevent picking up radioactive particles on their shoes and clothing. They also wear a mask over their nose and mouth to prevent breathing in radioactive dust.

Working in Chernobyl involves risk, but it is a risk researchers are willing to take to better understand the long-term effects of radiation on living things. "You cannot think about radiation all the time," Møller says," because there is work to be done!"

"Radiation might be destroying some of these pigment-producing cells directly."

Alternatively, the melanocytes could also be dying as a result of a phenomenon known as antioxidant depletion. Antioxidants are substances that protect cells from destructive molecules called free radicals. Vitamin E is a well-known antioxidant. Scientists have known for a long time that radiation causes free radicals to form in living things. The higher the amount of radiation to which an animal is exposed, the more free radicals are produced, forcing the animal's body to use more of its limited supply of antioxidants to repair free-radical damage. "We measured vitamin E and other antioxidants directly in the liver, blood, and eggs of barn swallows and found strong reductions, with the level of reduction increasing with the level of radiation," explained Møller.

However the melanocytes were being destroyed, Mousseau and Møller believed they had found clear evidence that radiation was harming barn swallows in the Zone. And patches of white feathers were just the beginning.

MORE ABNORMALITIES

After their first visit, Mousseau and Møller returned to Chernobyl every summer to study barn swallow populations in the Zone. They tracked the condition of individual birds and their offspring, year after year. After examining more than two thousand swallows from the Chernobyl region, the scientists concluded that radiation was doing much more than damaging melanocytes.

The scientists found barn swallows with deformed feet and toes and with misshapen beaks and eyes. Many birds have abnormally shaped feathers, such as tail feathers that curve or are much shorter on one side than the other. More disturbing are the swallows with tumors erupting from different parts of their bodies. Some of these cancerous lumps are large, measuring nearly 0.5 inch (1.3 centimeters) in diameter.

A significant number of swallows (and other birds in the Zone) also have cataracts, a condition in which the normally clear lens in the eye turns cloudy. Cataracts interfere with vision and eventually lead to blindness. Between 2011 and 2012, Mousseau and Møller examined at least twelve hundred birds living in different parts of the Zone for cataracts. Birds living in places with higher levels of background radiation had more cataracts than birds living where levels were lower.

The scientists have also discovered that many swallows in the Zone appear to be dying prematurely, when they are still quite young. "In natural, healthy populations of barn swallows," says Mousseau, "about 40 to 50 percent of the birds survive from one year to the next. In normal populations, it is not unusual to find birds that are three to five years old, while in Chernobyl, the probability of survival for swallows is only about 20 percent. Just one bird in four or five survives to the next year."

The two researchers are convinced radiation is responsible for the abnormalities and shortened life span. They believe their research has also revealed an unmistakable pattern: Barn swallows living in the most radioactively contaminated parts of the Zones are the most affected. In other words, the greater the radiation exposure, the more problems the birds have.

A male barn swallow (top) *from Chernobyl shows a high level of asymmetry in the length of its tail feathers. Mousseau and Møller think this abnormality is the result of stresses linked to radiation exposure. A cluster of rounded tumors* (bottom) *protrude from the underside of a nightingale captured at Chernobyl, also the likely result of radiation exposure.*

OTHER SPECIES IN TROUBLE

Mousseau and Møller have looked for signs of radiation damage in other species too. One discovery, Mousseau remembers, began with a chance observation about spiders. "When walking through woods in most parts of the world, you have to keep clearing cobwebs off your face because there are so many spiders. Around Chernobyl, we noticed relatively few cobwebs. So we started searching for spiders." He and Møller counted spiders at sites in different parts of the Zone. They found unusually small populations of spiders in most places. In hot spots, they found hardly any spiders at all.

In 2006 the scientists expanded their hunt to include insects as well as spiders. They began systematically counting insects in hundreds of locations, inside and—for comparison—outside the Zone. They counted butterflies, bumblebees, dragonflies, and grasshoppers. A familiar pattern soon emerged: the most radioactive sites had the lowest numbers of insects. Mousseau and Møller admit that in some places, factors besides radiation—such as food shortages or high numbers of predators—could be affecting insect and spider populations. Nevertheless, they suspect radiation is primarily to blame.

Another chance encounter suggested that radiation was causing mutations in insects in the Zone. While working one day, Møller happened to pick up a red fire bug. About the size of a fingernail, red fire bugs have a distinctive pattern of black spots and shapes on their bright red backs. Møller noticed the bug looked a little odd and realized it was missing a spot. He and Mousseau searched for and found more of the insects. Many of them had abnormal markings. The frequency of abnormal color patterns was highest in the more radioactive areas while most bugs in uncontaminated areas had normal color patterns. Because the pattern of spots is controlled by the fire bugs' DNA, the abnormalities suggested genetic mutations had occurred.

The scientists admit they would need to do laboratory experiments to confirm that radiation and not something else caused the mutations. Yet, these insects spend critical times during their development (as eggs and larvae) in soil that is heavily contaminated

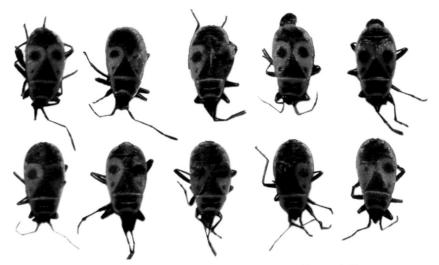

These are just a few of many fire bugs collected by Møller and Mousseau at Chernobyl that display irregular spot and coloration patterns, a sign of genetic mutations that the scientists believe were caused by radiation damage to the insects' DNA.

with mutation-inducing radionuclides. Odds are good, the scientists believe, that radiation is the cause.

FOOTPRINTS TELL A STORY

Thriving. Abundant. Flourishing. For years, articles in newspapers and magazines—some written by scientists—have used such words to describe wildlife in the Exclusion Zone. It is perhaps true that more wolves, foxes, deer, and other kinds of large mammals live inside the Zone than outside its boundary fences. But Mousseau and Møller wondered if wildlife was truly abundant everywhere in the Zone, including the most radioactive places.

"Most reports of abundance are anecdotal," says Mousseau, "based on personal accounts rather than facts." Even Sergey Gaschak admits this is true. In the Ukrainian portion of the Zone, at least, no one has carried out a scientific census of large mammals recently.

In the winter of 2009, Mousseau and Møller decided to take a census. They used a technique that ecologists all over the world employ to estimate the size of wildlife populations: they counted animal tracks in the snow. The two scientists staked out 161 transects, or long straight paths, each 328 feet (100 m) long through forests,

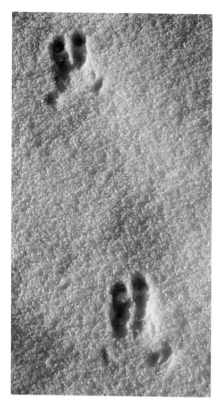

Scientists Mousseau and Møller identified and counted tracks in the snow during a census they made of large mammals in the Zone. These are the tracks of a wild boar.

meadows, and other kinds of habitats in the Zone. Some of the sites were in places where radiation levels were high, and some were where it was relatively low.

After a fresh snowfall, the scientists hurried to the transects. They counted 445 tracks made by a dozen different species of mammals. The majority of the tracks, however, belonged to only a few species: red foxes, wolves, and hare. The scientists found noticeably fewer tracks along transects that ran through high-radiation sites. Large mammals, at least, were not at all abundant.

STILL NOT CLEAR

For more than a quarter century, scientists have been collecting small snapshots of what has been happening in the Chernobyl Exclusion Zone. But the big picture remains incomplete and confusing. Different teams of researchers have reached very different conclusions about the effects of the background radiation on life in the Zone. Some scientists, including Mousseau and Møller, are at one end of the spectrum. Based on their findings, the two men are convinced chronic, low-level radiation is harming many, if not most, of the animals. Other researchers, including Baker and his colleagues at Texas Tech, maintain that radiation's impact on wildlife in the Zone may be positive in some cases, by stimulating cells to protect themselves more effectively from radiation damage. In other cases, radiation's effects, while negative, are believed to be not significant enough to impact populations of animals.

BAKER'S LATEST RESULTS

In 2011 Baker and his colleagues returned to Chernobyl and collected bank voles from some of the same sites where they had collected voles in 1996. Because voles tend to live and breed in the same area year after year, the researchers assumed that the newly captured bank voles were likely the descendants of the vole populations they had encountered fifteen years earlier.

The researchers took cell samples from the newly captured voles and compared them to cells taken and frozen for preservation from the 1996 voles. Rather than looking for mutations in the DNA in the nuclei of the cells, however, Baker and his team analyzed DNA in tiny cell organelles known as mitochondria. Mitochondria are the structures that turn chemical energy from food into energy that cells can use to power everything they do. Mitochondrial DNA (mtDNA) is a much smaller and less complicated molecule than nuclear DNA, making it easier to work with.

The Baker team compared the mtDNA of the newly captured voles to the mtDNA of the 1996 voles. Lo and behold, they found mutations—but only in voles from the most highly radioactive locations within the Zone. Baker's conclusion? "What we discovered is that the animals from the radioactive sites do have altered genomes [mutations in their mtDNA]. Altered, we believe, as a consequence of living in one of the most radioactive regions of Chernobyl. But only after almost forty bank vole generations."

Baker concludes that while some of these mtDNA mutations are probably harmful, they have not had an obvious effect on the voles in the Red Forest. The vole population is still large and apparently thriving. And the voles, he says, "still look normal."

Making sense of such opposing viewpoints is not easy. But science is rarely straightforward. Experiments don't often lead to quick, clear answers and tidy results. That is especially true when studying animals and plants. It is likely that different species respond to radiation in different ways. Changes such as genetic mutations may take a long time to show up. Teasing out the effects of radiation when other variables, such as food shortages or large numbers of predators, could be playing a role is also difficult. "The most important thing we've learned so far

Members of Timothy Mousseau's research team are covered from head to toe in protective gear as they walk through a part of the Red Forest in the Exclusion Zone.

is just how little we understand about the role played by low-level, low-dose radiation in natural environments," says Mousseau.

Doing research in the Chernobyl Exclusion Zone is difficult. To some people, it might seem like a waste of time. After all, the nuclear accident that created the Zone occurred decades ago. Why do scientists return to do research year after year? Why do they arm themselves with dosimeters, put on protective clothing, and spend weeks tramping through a place where the radioactivity could be a risk to their health?

They do it because what is happening to Chernobyl's wildlife could happen again. In fact, it already has.

CHAPTER 5

LEARNING FROM CHERNOBYL

Experts in the nuclear power industry blamed Chernobyl's nuclear meltdown on human error and a poorly designed nuclear reactor. The disaster was a fluke, some said—a once-in-a-lifetime event. According to their reports, it was very unlikely that a major nuclear accident could happen again.

On March 11, 2011, it did.

An extremely powerful undersea earthquake occurred off the Pacific coast of Honshu, Japan's largest island. It was the fifth most powerful earthquake ever recorded. The quake triggered an enormous tsunami. Roughly an hour after the earthquake shook the island, a series of gigantic waves struck Honshu's northeastern coast, surging as far as 6 miles (10 km) inland. Roads buckled and buildings collapsed. Cars, trucks, ships, and trains were tossed around like toys. Entire towns were churned into rubble and then swept away as the water rushed back out to sea. More than nineteen thousand people lost their lives.

The Fukushima Daiichi nuclear power plant, along the coast just south of the worst destruction, lost electrical power when the earthquake severed the plant's connection to Japan's national power grid. Emergency generators came on to supply electricity to the pumps that circulated coolant water around the reactor cores. When the tsunami struck, however, seawater flooded the buildings that housed the reactors. The submerged generators sputtered and died. Coolant water stopped flowing, the reactors overheated, and their cores began to melt. Explosions rocked three of Fukushima's nuclear reactors, releasing a cloud of radioactive particles, including iodine-131, cesium-137, strontium-90, and other dangerous radionuclides. As the nuclear fallout drifted over the surrounding countryside, radiation levels soared. Close to the plant, they topped 170 mSv per hour.

The radioactive material released from Fukushima's reactors was about one-tenth the amount released from Chernobyl's Reactor Number 4. Nevertheless, the accident ranks as the world's second-largest nuclear power plant disaster on record. Prevailing winds swept

The 2011 earthquake off the coast of northeastern Japan triggered enormous waves such as this one, which crashed over a seawall in Miyako the day of the quake. The waves swamped the Fukushima Daiichi nuclear power plant in the area, leading to a nuclear meltdown.

OCEAN IMPACTS

A few days after the Fukushima accident, highly radioactive coolant water stored in tanks near the reactors began leaking into the Pacific Ocean. Engineers tried unsuccessfully to stop the leaks. By August 2013, at least 300 tons (272 metric tons) of contaminated water had made its way into the sea. This massive discharge of radioactive water, combined with the radioactive fallout released during the initial explosions in 2011, has created the largest discharge of radioactivity into the ocean ever recorded. Vast numbers of bottom-dwelling fish and other ocean animals along Japan's Pacific coast are now contaminated with high levels of cesium-137. Government officials have banned fishing near Fukushima.

much of the nuclear fallout out over the Pacific Ocean. Still, fallout contaminated 11,580 square miles (30,000 sq. km) of land and forced the evacuation of 160,000 people. The Japanese government declared an area with a radius of 12 miles (20 km) from the power plant to be too radioactive for human habitation. Almost overnight, the world had another Exclusion Zone.

RADIATION DÉJÀ VU

As soon as Fukushima's damaged reactors were stabilized, scientists arrived to begin assessing the impact of the disaster. They determined from soil and seawater samples that Fukushima's explosions had released fifty types of radionuclides into the environment, including huge amounts of cesium-137. The researchers calculated that in the first thirty days after the accident, animals and plants near the power plant, as well as fish and marine algae offshore, received radiation doses several thousand times above safe limits.

A team of researchers from Japan's Okinawa University found evidence of damage from that exposure within two months of the accident. They collected dozens of small pale grass blue butterflies near the Fukushima power plant and from uncontaminated sites in other parts of the country. When the accident occurred, the butterflies were in the larval (caterpillar) stage of their life cycle. Those living near Fukushima had eaten plants dusted with nuclear fallout and had crawled over radionuclide-contaminated ground.

The butterflies the scientists collected from uncontaminated sites looked normal. Those from Fukushima had deformed wings, antennae, and legs. The abnormalities were clear signs of radiation-induced genetic mutations that had occurred in the butterflies while they were still in the caterpillar stage.

The Japanese scientists then bred the deformed butterflies they had collected from around Fukushima to produce a second generation. These offspring had more—and more severe—deformities than their parents. The mutations caused by radiation in the first generation had been passed on to the next.

In the months and years following the Fukushima disaster, scientists from all over the world have

Scientists studied abnormalities among pale grass blue butterflies, which are common in Japan, after the Fukushima nuclear disaster. Among many things, they noticed a range of abnormal spot patterns on the wings of successive generations of the butterflies, including deletion, addition, enlargement, and fusion of spots. From this, they concluded that the radiation released from the damaged nuclear power plant had led to genetic damage in the butterfly population.

come to study the ongoing impacts of radiation on the wildlife there. Beginning in the summer of 2011, Timothy Mousseau and Anders Møller have visited Fukushima's exclusion zone every summer to carry out many of the same types of studies they have been doing in Chernobyl. They have seen similar signs of radiation damage in animals from both sites. In places with high levels of radiation, for example, the researchers found significantly fewer than normal numbers of birds, spiders, and insects. And they have spotted barn swallows with patches of white feathers.

Chernobyl—and now Fukushima—are unique natural laboratories where scientists can study the effects of radiation on individual species as well as on complex communities of living things. It is important research that needs to continue. "Not everyone should go to Chernobyl [or Fukushima]," says Robert Baker, "but someone should. We need to know what is happening there." Despite their differing conclusions about radiation's effects on living things, Baker, Mousseau, Møller, and other scientists working at Chernobyl and Fukushima do agree on one thing: the more we know about the impact of radiation on living things in their natural environment, the better prepared we will be for the next accident—which may happen sooner than we think.

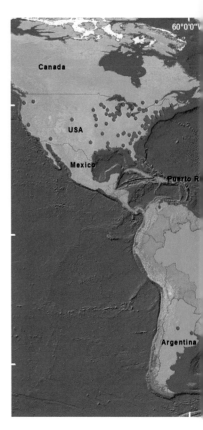

A NUCLEAR FUTURE?

According to the World Nuclear Association, 432 electricity-generating nuclear reactors were in operation around the globe in 2013. Several dozen new ones were under construction. Currently, the United States has the most nuclear power plants of any nation. Other countries with large numbers of reactors include France, Russia, Japan, and India.

As the world's population grows, so does the need for energy, especially electricity. Nuclear reactors generate about 13 percent of the electricity used worldwide. Much of the rest comes from power plants that burn fossil fuels such as oil, coal, and natural gas. Burning fossil fuels has become a serious environment problem, however, because it releases huge amounts of the gas carbon dioxide. In the atmosphere, carbon dioxide traps heat radiating from Earth's surface that would otherwise escape into space. The more carbon dioxide in the atmosphere, the more heat is trapped. The result is global warming, an increase in Earth's average surface temperature.

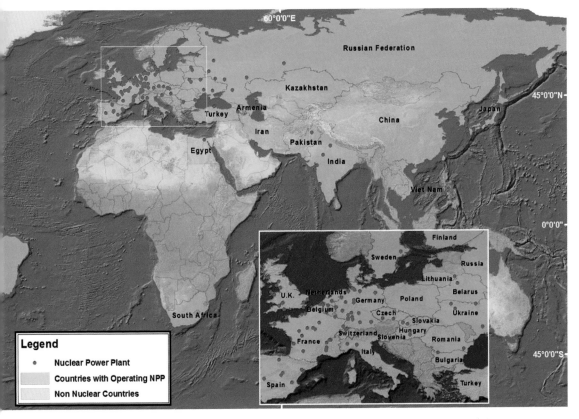

Legend
- Nuclear Power Plant
- Countries with Operating NPP
- Non Nuclear Countries

This global map by the United Nations Environment Programme shows the distribution of nuclear power plants around the world. Plants are concentrated in developed parts of the world such as western Europe and the United States.

Since the 1950s, scientists have documented a steady increase in carbon dioxide levels in the atmosphere. Earth's average temperature has increased by several degrees during that time. A growing body of evidence suggests that this worldwide warming is changing Earth's climate. Polar ice caps and mountain glaciers are melting. Sea levels are rising. Extreme weather events, from hurricanes and heat waves to floods and droughts, are becoming more common.

To combat global warming, countries around the world are looking for ways to generate electricity without burning fossil fuels. Renewable energy sources such as solar, wind, and water power are possible options. However, when the sun doesn't shine or the wind doesn't blow, electricity production slows or stops. Nuclear power plants, on the other hand, can produce an uninterrupted supply of electricity while releasing relatively little carbon dioxide. Many people believe nuclear power plants are the best answer to solving the world's growing need for electricity while keeping carbon dioxide emissions—and climate change—to a minimum. With nuclear power plants, though, comes the risk of nuclear meltdowns and the release of dangerous ionizing radiation. And that risk is growing.

In 2012 scientists at Germany's Max Planck Institute for Chemistry announced that the likelihood of a nuclear accident such as those at Chernobyl and Fukushima has been underestimated for a long time. According to their calculations, they believe a nuclear reactor disaster will occur somewhere in the world every ten to twenty years. The researchers also ran computer simulations to show the potential impact of such accidents in different parts of the world. A nuclear meltdown in western Europe, for instance, could potentially threaten 28 million people with some level of radiation exposure. In southern Asia, where population densities are even greater, a major nuclear accident could affect 34 million people.

One lesson the world has learned from Chernobyl and Fukushima is that the unexpected can and does happen. The residents of Pripyat never imagined that the reactors they saw from their windows every day would become a threat. But a test gone wrong changed their minds—and their lives—forever. The Fukushima Daiichi power plant was built to withstand powerful earthquakes and even tsunami waves—up to 18.7 feet (5.7 m) high. Yet some of the waves that struck the power plant in 2011 were more than 50 feet (15 m) high. The result was another nuclear disaster and a radioactive legacy that will linger for decades, perhaps centuries to come.

If the world's energy future becomes increasingly nuclear, scientists need to learn a lot more about the long-term effects of radiation exposure on living things following a nuclear accident. Learning how radiation affects plants and animals is crucial, because however it affects them is also how it will affect us.

LIFE WILL FIND A WAY

Chernobyl is teaching us another important lesson: the remarkable resilience of life on Earth. Although it is too early to tell at Fukushima, most species of animals and plants in Chernobyl's

A raven stretches its wings atop a sign warning of radiation hazards in the Exclusion Zone. While a diverse array of animal and plant life has survived and reproduced since the disaster, the long-term consequences are still not clear.

Exclusion Zone survived the nuclear accident. Individuals may have died, but populations of living things have reclaimed the land. Some species seem to have emerged largely untouched by the invisible radiation that still surrounds them. Others show negative effects, but with time, they may successfully adapt to a world where relatively high levels of background radiation is the norm for many decades. Only time—and scientific investigations—will tell.

In short, life has carried on. While scientists continue piecing together the full story of what is happening in the shadow of Reactor Number 4, the animals that creep and scamper and swim and soar through the abandoned lands around it will go on living as best they can in the radioactive kingdom they call home.

AUTHOR'S NOTE

I remember Chernobyl. I remember the television news reports of radiation clouds. I remember seeing a satellite photo of the power plant taken three days after the accident and the tiny red dot of the still-burning reactor. The fact that plants and animals have made such a seemingly dramatic recovery in the Exclusion Zone is amazing to me. So is the complexity of radiation's impact on living things. So is the fact that most young people I talk to when I visit schools have never heard of Chernobyl. They need to.

This book would not have been possible without the kind assistance of a number of scientists who took time from their busy schedules to talk with me, share their experiences, answer innumerable questions, provide detailed explanations of difficult topics, and make available their personal photographs. In particular, I would like to thank Dr. Timothy Mousseau of the University of South Carolina; Dr. Anders Pape Møller of the Université Paris–Sud in Orsay, France; Dr. Robert J. Baker of Texas Tech University; and Dr. Sergey Gaschak of the International Radioecology Laboratory in Slavutych, Ukraine. In addition, I appreciate the contribution made by Dr. Jeffrey Wickliffe of Tulane University who, along with Robert Baker, converted the radiation dose received by bank voles in the Red Forest into a (terrifying) human equivalent.

Last but not at all least, I want to thank my readers. The world rests in your hands.

GLOSSARY

biodiversity: the variety of living things in a place or region

DNA: deoxyribonucleic acid, the molecule found in the nucleus of cells of every living thing that contains the genetic instructions for building and maintaining that organism

dosimeter: an instrument that measures a person's exposure to ionizing radiation

fallout: airborne radioactive particles that gradually fall to Earth as dust or in rain or snow

half-life: the time it takes for half a given amount of a radionuclide to undergo radioactive decay into a different form or element

hormesis (hohr-MEE-sihs): the hypothesis that relatively small amounts of something harmful, such as ionizing radiation, may be helpful to living things by making their cells more resistant to damage or disease

ionizing radiation: energy waves or atomic particles powerful enough to damage molecules in the cells of living things; for example, by producing mutations in DNA

mitochondria: organelles (tiny structures) inside cells that convert energy into a form readily usable by cells; one of these structures is called a mitochondrion

mitochondrial DNA (mtDNA): a small DNA molecule found in mitochondria that contains genetic instructions necessary for mitochondria to function properly

mutation: a change in the genetic instructions in a living thing's DNA

orthnithologist: a biologist who specializes in studying birds

radioactive: able to release ionizing radiation

radioactive decay: when the unstable nucleus of a radionuclide spontaneously breaks down and emits ionizing radiation in the form of energy waves or atomic particles

radionuclide: an atom with an unstable nucleus that can undergo radioactive decay and emit ionizing radiation

SOURCE NOTES

11 Vitaly Petrenko, "Cross-Country Race in the Red Forest: Pripyat Teenagers and the Catastrophe," *Pripyat.com*, accessed May 20, 2013, http://pripyat.com/en/articles/cross-country-race-red-forest-pripyat-teenagers-and-catastrophe.html

19 Sergey Gaschak, personal communication with the author, July 12–14, 2013.

25 Chernobyl Forum: 2003–2005, "Chernobyl's Legacy: Health, Environmental, and Socio-Economic Impacts and Recommendations to the Governments of Belarus, the Russian Federation and Ukraine," *IAEA.org*, accessed May 3, 2013, http://www.iaea.org/Publications/Booklets/Chernobyl/chernobyl.pdf, 29.

26 Holly Morris, "The Women Living in Chernobyl's Toxic Wasteland," *Telegraph*, November 8, 2012, accessed August 2, 2013, http://www.telegraph.co.uk/earth/environment/9646437/The-women-living-in-Chernobyls-toxic-wasteland.html.

27 Gaschak, personal communication with the author.

28 Robert J. Baker, personal communication with the author, August 15, 2013.

28–29 Ibid.

29 Ibid.

32 Ibid.

33 Ibid.

33 Ibid.

36–37 Timothy Mousseau, personal communication with the author, April 24, 2013.

38 Anders Møller, personal communication with the author, May 20–21, 2013.

38 Timothy Mousseau, personal communication with the author, December 20, 2013.

38–39 Mousseau, personal communication with the author, April 24, 2013.

39 Møller, personal communication with the author, May 20–21, 2013.

39 Ibid.

39 Møller, personal communication with the author, January 23, 2014.

40 Mousseau, personal communication with the author, April 24, 2013.

42 Ibid.

43 Ibid.

45 Baker, personal communication with the author.

45 Ibid.

46–47 Steven Powell, "Fukushima, Two Years Later," *SC.edu*, March 11, 2013, accessed July 28, 2103, http://www.sc.edu/news/newsarticle.php?nid=6079#.Uhfl2hvOmSo.

52 Baker, personal communication with the author.

SELECTED BIBLIOGRAPHY

Baker, Robert J., Meredith J. Hamilton, Ronald A. Den Bussche, Lara E. Wiggins, Derrick W. Sugg, Michael H. Smith, D. Lomakin, Sergey P. Gaschak, Elena G. Bundova, Galena A. Rudenskaya, and Ronald K. Chesser. "Small Mammals from the Most Radioactive Sites Near the Chornobyl Nuclear Power Plant." *Journal of Mammalogy* 77 (1996): 155–170.

Bird, Winifred A., and Jane Braxton Little. "A Tale of Two Forests: Addressing Postnuclear Radiation at Chernobyl and Fukushima." *Environmental Health Perspectives* 121 (2013): 78–85. Accessed September 5, 2013. http://ehp.niehs.nih.gov/pdf-files/2013/Mar/ehp.121-a78_508.pdf.

Chernobyl Forum: 2003–2005, "Chernobyl's Legacy: Health, Environmental, and Socio-Economic Impacts and Recommendations to the Governments of Belarus, the Russian Federation and Ukraine." *IAEA.org.* Accessed May 3, 2013. http://www.iaea.org/Publications/Booklets/Chernobyl/chernobyl.pdf.

Chesser, Ronald K., and Robert J. Baker. "Growing Up with Chernobyl." *American Scientist* 94 (2006): 542–549.

Cottingham, Katie. "Proteomics of Chernobyl-Grown Seeds Gives Hints about Adaptation to Radiation." *Journal of Proteome Research*, May 5, 2009. Accessed August 31, 2013. http://pubs.acs.org/action/showStoryContent?doi=10.1021%2F on.2009.05.04.363768&.

Featherstone, Steve. "Life in the Zone." *Harper's Magazine*, June 2011, 41–48.

Higginbotham, Adam. "Is Chernobyl a Wild Kingdom or a Radioactive Den of Decay?" *Wired*, May 2011, 157–167.

Hiyama, Atsuki, Chiyo Nohara, Seira Kinjo, Wataru Taira, Shinichi Gima, Akira Tanahara, and Joji M. Otaki. "The Biological Impacts of the Fukushima Nuclear Accident on the Pale Grass Blue Butterfly." *Scientific Reports* 2 (August 2012): 1–10. Accessed August 12, 2013. http://www.nature.com/srep/2012/120809/srep00570/pdf/srep00570.pdf.

Lelieveld, J., D. Kunkel, and M. G. Lawrence. "Global Risk of Radioactive Fallout after Major Nuclear Reactor Accidents." *Atmospheric Chemistry and Physics* 12 (2012): 4245–4258. Accessed August 3, 2013. http://www.atmos-chem-phys.net/12/4245/2012/acp-12-4245-2012.html.

Møller, Anders Pape, and Timothy A. Mousseau. "Assessing Effects of Radiation on Abundance of Mammals and Predator–Prey Interactions in Chernobyl Using Tracks in the Snow." *Ecological Indicators* 26 (2013): 112–116.

———. "Biological Consequences of Chernobyl: 20 Years On." *Trends in Ecology and Evolution* 21 (2006): 200–207. Accessed April 10, 2013. http://cricket.biol.sc.edu/chernobyl/papers/Moller-Mousseau-TREE-2006-PR1.pdf.

———. "The Effects of Low-Dose Radiation." *Significance* 10 (February 2013): 14–19. Accessed May 14, 2013. http://onlinelibrary.wiley.com/doi/10.1111/j.1740-9713.2013.00630.x/pdf.

Møller, Anders Pape, Timothy A. Mousseau, F. de Lope, and N. Saino. "Anecdotes and Empirical Research in Chernobyl." *Biology Letters* 4 (2008): 65–66. Accessed September 2, 2013. http://rsbl.royalsocietypublishing.org/content/4/1/65.full.pdf+html.

————. "Elevated Frequency of Abnormalities in Barn Swallows from Chernobyl." *Biology Letters* 3 (2007): 414–417. Accessed April 3, 2013. http://rsbl.royalsocietypublishing .org/content/3/4/414.full.pdf+html.

Mousseau, Timothy A., and Anders Pape Møller. "Entomological Studies in Chernobyl and Fukushima." *American Entomologist* 58 (2012): 148–150. Accessed April 22, 2013. http://cricket.biol.sc.edu/chernobyl/papers/Mousseal-Moller-AE-2012.pdf.

————. "Landscape Portrait: A Look at the Impacts of Radioactive Contaminants on Chernobyl's Wildlife." *Bulletin of the Atomic Scientists* 67 (2011): 38–46. Accessed February 1, 2013. http://thebulletin.org/2011/marchapril/landscape-portrait-look -impacts-radioactive-contaminants-chernobyl%E2%80%99s-wildlife.

Peplow, Mark. "Chernobyl's Legacy." *Nature* 471 (2011): 562–565.

Rodgers, Brenda E., and Kristen M. Holmes. "Radio-Adaptive Response to Environmental Exposures at Chernobyl." *Dose-Response* 6 (2008): 209–221.

Shukman, Henry. "Chernobyl, My Primeval, Teeming, Irradiated Eden." *Outside Online Magazine*, February 15, 2011. Accessed July 20, 2013. http://www.outsideonline.com /outdoor-adventure/science/Chernobyl--My-Primeval--Teeming--Irradiated-Eden .html?page=all.

"What Is Radiation?" World Nuclear Association, 2014. Accessed February 22, 2013. http://www.world-nuclear.org/Nuclear-Basics/What-is-radiation-/.

FOR FURTHER INFORMATION

Books

Alexievich, Svetlana. *Voices from Chernobyl: The Oral History of a Nuclear Disaster*. New York: Picador, 2006. This landmark book contains a collection of firsthand accounts from Chernobyl survivors of all ages—their experiences during and after the nuclear accident and its effect on their lives.

Blackwell, Andrew. *Visit Sunny Chernobyl: And Other Adventures in the World's Most Polluted Places*. Emmaus, PA: Rodale Books, 2012. In the first chapter of this candidly written book, the author shares his experience visiting Chernobyl and the Exclusion Zone more than twenty-five years after the disaster.

Bortz, Fred. *Meltdown! The Nuclear Disaster in Japan and Our Energy Future*. Minneapolis: Twenty-First Century Books, 2012. This book examines the human tragedy and the scientific implications of the nuclear meltdown in Japan in 2011 and explores the global debate about the future of nuclear power and alternative sources of energy.

Brennan, Kristine. *The Chernobyl Nuclear Disaster*. New York: Chelsea House, 2002. This book offers a clear, concise summary of the Chernobyl nuclear accident and its immediate aftermath.

Doeden, Matt. *Green Energy: Crucial Gains or Economic Strains?* Minneapolis: Twenty-First Century Books, 2010. This title examines the pros and cons of renewable energy, with a chapter specifically devoted to the debate surrounding nuclear energy.

Medvedev, Grigori. *The Truth about Chernobyl*. London: I. B. Tauris, 1991. A compelling, minute-by-minute account of the events leading up to the meltdown of Chernobyl's Reactor Number 4, this book was written by a Soviet nuclear engineer intimately familiar with the reactor and the accident. It is a challenging read but worth it.

Mycio, Mary. *Wormwood Forest: A Natural History of Chernobyl*. Washington, DC: Joseph Henry Press, 2005. This book is a nonscientist's impression of Chernobyl's impacts based on interviews with Chernobyl survivors and self-settlers and on encounters with wildlife in the Zone.

Websites and Videos

"The Chernobyl Disaster: 25 Years Ago." In Focus with Alan Taylor. *Atlantic*, March 23, 2011. http://www.theatlantic.com/infocus/2011/03/the-chernobyl-disaster-25-years-ago/100033/. This website contains a collection of photos assembled at the time of the twenty-fifth anniversary of the Chernobyl nuclear accident that provides at in-depth glimpse into the disaster and its aftermath.

Chernobyl: Life in the Dead Zone. Daily Motion video. 49:05. From a Discovery Channel broadcast. Posted by "bobi98," May 12, 2012. http://www.dailymotion.com/video/xqsafw_chernobyl-life-in-the-dead-zone_shortfilms. This Discovery Channel film relates the story of the Chernobyl disaster and the wildlife recovery in the Exclusion Zone.

"Evacuation of Pripyat." YouTube video clip. 4:44. Posted by "Kekszbab," July 19, 2008. http://www.youtube.com/watch?v=FrhLueO_Iho&feature=related. Footage for this video was shot in Pripyat on the days surrounding the Chernobyl power plant disaster in April 1986.

Fukushima Daiichi Nuclear Disaster Video. YouTube video. 49:23. Posted by "Jayadevan TR," June 18, 2013. http://www.youtube.com/watch?v=rsozk925QWg&list=TLVnk8pvlGB8w. A documentary that explores the details of the Fukushima Daiichi disaster in 2011, this video includes reenactments of events that took place inside the power plant.

"Is Chernobyl's Wildlife Really Thriving?" BBC video. 2:46. Narrated by Victoria Gill. Video available in "Chernobyl's Legacy Recorded in Trees." August 8, 2013. http://www.bbc.co.uk/news/science-environment-23619870. Watch scientists Timothy Mousseau and his colleagues examine birds caught and released as part of their recent research activities in the Exclusion Zone.

Radioactive Wolves. PBS video. 53:10. October 19, 2011. http://video.pbs.org/video/2157025070/. This documentary focuses on wolf packs inside Chernobyl's Exclusion Zone and the scientists who are studying them.

INDEX